WESTWARD UNDER VEGA

Thomas Wood Stevens

WEST=
WARD
UNDER
VEGA

New York : Covici · Friede

TO HELEN

Stan and Mary please write.

WESTWARD UNDER VEGA

IN *spring, along the Magdalena road,*
They take Ysidro, the good farmer's saint,
Into the fields to bless the crops to come.
Ysidro, in a hundred images
Immanent, looks through twice a hundred eyes
Painted on oak that came no one knows when
From Spain, or on white poplar root, new-carved
Like a new Hopi doll, across the fields
And gives his benison. Things do not change
Along the Magdalena road. And for
The good saint's day they make a festival.
The herders from the upland ranges come
To swell the small devout processionals,
For lambing time is over, and each man
Brings to his caporal *the full spring count,*
For on this day he knows that San Ysidro
Will mediate a sheepman's prayer as soon
As any farmer's letting water in
From the acequeias *on the thirsty land.*
And it is good, when lambing time is over
And the last ewe's stained shivering lambs
Are gathered up, to reckon what the spring

9

Has yielded, just what ewes are dry,
How many more will bear another year,
How many wethers will November yield
Ready for slaughter. . . . Count and count again.

You'll have to pledge the flock for money soon
To pay the shearers. Till you sell your wool
The banker at Socorro will have more
To say than San Ysidro. Count them well.

So many clerks in Washington, and keys
For clerks to strike, and intricate wheels
To click and check and sum the counting up:
For each ten years the careful Government
Must know how many souls, how many mouths
To feed, how many bodies to be housed,
There are between the oceans. Row on row
The quick machines are clicking up the count,
And men feed in the answers from the rolls,
Vital statistics, children born, households
Of this or that creed, color, race and trade,
Owning their homes, or not—in all sixteen
Impertinent questions asked and facts ticked off
By census takers up and down the land.
They make you reel, these totals, if you let
Your mind rest on the people, women, men,
Children, adults, black people, red and white,
Households, and mouths to feed, and mortgages,
And fires to build o' mornings. . . .
But if you were a census office clerk
Like John, and pressed the keys of a machine,
Or April, who just filed the yellow sheets

When John had totaled them, you got to know
That these were only papers, numbers, names,
Not living souls—they were too far away—
No pulse in them—no moment in their answers.

But if John said, as April passed, "Say now,
Will you be home tonight?"—and she said, "Yes,"
There was a question with a stake in it,
An answer with a whirl of joy behind.

THERE was a matter of a poker game
The night before the job gave out, a night
When April had said "No" and John was reckless.
And that night John by some luck held a straight,
Queen high, and Slim, whose job was also gone,
Slim drew three kings and backed them with his shirt.
The others all fell out. "I'll raise you five,"
John dropped from iron lips. "I'm flat,"
Slim said, "but I'll put up the Ford."
The others laughed. They'd hardly say Slim called,
Knowing the Ford, but John let down his hand.
And as Slim dropped his three kings on the table
John felt behind his iron poker face
A flushing as of sunshine, and a streaming
Of long green hills and rivers blazing by,
And Kansas, and the first bright gleam of snow
On mountains that stood sharp against the sunset;
And April was on all the hills and prairies,
And at the foot of all those velvet mountains,
And on their summits, looking to the west. . . .

"Right, Horace Greeley," John said solemnly.
The sunset faded and the stars came out.
And Slim said, "Nerts. But maybe you can make
The damn thing run. I couldn't. Well, so long."

ONE hundred dollars and a Model T,
That was their fortune—if you'd call it that—
Their passport to the opening westward road—
The sum of all that John and April had.
There were some other items, yes. Six books
Of verse, a map o' the stars, a compass, not
So accurate as it might have been, some tools
And a surveyor's kit for—who can tell—
You might by good luck find a gold mine there
In the far West where the great spaces lie,
And you'd as well stake out your claim by rule,
Not trusting to Polaris for your bounds.
And if you found a gold mine, then you'd need
A pick and shovel; they were tied across
And helped to hold the bumper-rod together
Where it was broken. That was all they had
To start with. Later on they lost the compass,
And acquired—five dollars went for it—
A document, set forth in legal terms
With both their names, and a device of doves
And roses, from a Justice of the Peace.

Out on the Cumberland Pike,
Step on the gas, my lad!
Never a key to strike,
Never a sum to add,
But a road through the Maryland hills awinding
And the wind in your face and the sunset blinding.

Road where the wagon trains
Long ago to the West
Wound in the wintry rains
Over the bloody crest,
And the redcoats marched through the mud and the
sleet
And the sodden drums were too slackened to beat.

Here was where Stuart spurred
Under the stars and bars—
Dixie the tune they heard—
Gray-coated avatars
To the bridge by the forges, the hunger and trouble,
To the field of Antietam—to death—at the double!

Out on the Cumberland Pike,
Road now of joyous love,
Over canal and dike
Up to the hills above,

And the five green mountains to cross and climb
With pulses singing and hearts in rhyme.

    Step on the gas, my lad,
        (Fools—young fools at the wheel)
    Luck may be good or bad:
        Life strikes the flint and steel:
But the Cumberland Pike is the road to follow
From Washington west. . . . It's my road, Apollo.

IN West Virginia, up from Berkeley Springs
That night, the one-eyed Ford went blind
And John swung off the highway in a pasture
That smelled of violets, faintly, in the dark.
"Far as we go," John said, and April, "Check,"
Though never in her guarded maiden life
Had she so faced the unsheltering firmament.
They lay upon the grass, and saw above
The Lyre, and steel-bright Vega swinging clear
Of the dim tree-tops, and saw Mars go down
Gold in the dark leaves following the moon.
They had not planned for this.   They had no plan.
They had not talked of it, nor talked at all,
Save as a thing apart from them, of love.
But now they talked, low-voiced and hungrily,
About the constellations, greeting them
As they so slowly drifted up the sky
In the warm night. She crushed a violet cluster
Beneath her hair, and the full scent came rich
Into her breath. The stars were very near.
But while she half-way lifted up her head
To mark where Sagittarius swung free

From the black leafage to the south, she knew
The secret stars would never scorn, nor break
Their lonely silences. She loved the stars.
Then, "John," she whispered, and his head, so near,
Blotted out Vega, blotted all the stars,
And their lips clung, and would not come apart.

Drink-in the night
For here is such a wine
As fills you with a drunkenness divine
And sweeps the world into your ken and power
And gives the god-illusion to the hour.

Drink-in the night
And feel the beat of it,
The glory and the sweet of it,
The violets crushed and the enfolding rose,
The arms that cling and lips on lips that close.

Drink-in the night:
The earth is under you,
And all its fullness there to wonder you;
You're lordly while you hear the whip-poor-will;
(Thank God for sleep before that bird is still.)

Drink-in the night
For when your breast and hers
Press close, the god within you stirs—
Then you can saddle the wild clouds and ride
(But they'll throw you in the morning)
And pluck the stars and give them to the bride—
(Who am I to cry you warning?)

Drink-in the night.
The morning dews are chill,
And Love, who has so warm and sweet a will,
He'll shrink and whine and shiver when the wise
Gray Dawn puts silver pennies on his eyes.

IT was not their idea to pick him up—
The sailor hiking home to Uniontown. 'Twas his.
But April that day learned to drive the Ford
And the perverse mechanic thing would charge
At any spot she fixed her eyes upon,
And that damned sailor with his shiny suitcase
Could not be passed, and so she killed the engine.
"Thanks, sister," said the sailor, throwing in
The shiny suitcase on their camping kit;
And John got out and cranked, and took the wheel,
Not too well pleased. "Where are you headed for?"
The sailor asked. "Just west," said John. The sun,
Low hung, dazzled his eyes from the bright road.
She felt John's body close upon her left
And that was good. But on her right the sailor
Somehow was just as close, and not so good.

"I knew a girl in Porto Rico once—
A pippin she was, like you as two peas.
Not so good-looking, though. I fell for her
And she for me." "Where are you bound," John
    asked.

"Why Uniontown." "It's off our road." "I'll stick
If you don't mind, with you—up to the cross-road.
Say, buddy, you're in luck." And he was looking
Not at John, but April. "Got any grub?"
"A little." "I could eat." He shared their supper
Where they had lit a fire beside a stream
And talked the while of tropic ports and islands
And places farther from the sun-washed West
Than hell from heaven. His appraising glance
Measured up John with his wan office pallor
Touched with the one day's sunburn. Then a silence.
"How long you two been married?" Suddenly
He sprung the question. A blank moment passed.
"I thought so," said the sailor. And his eyes
Narrowed and lighted. "Girlie, listen here.
Just take a walk with me into the woods
And I'll be good to you—while he washes up."
John rose, and took the shiny suitcase down
And set it in the road. "Aw, what the hell——"
And John said nothing. But he ducked in time.

At the next county seat they routed out
A sleepy and not over-willing clerk;
And in the morning, with one eye mouse-colored,

And swollen knuckles on his right, John led
April, surrendering, to the Justice's.

Epithalamium on the Cumberland Pike. . . .
Who sings—who sings?
My voice is cracked
But I hear wings
Lifting along the clouded azure like
The doves that nest on Paphos, and racked
As I am with years, I'll swing
My wheezy concertina in the praise
Of wedded love, and happy nights and days.

I've driven along on the Cumberland Pike
In shine and in rain,
And I'll sing it's just as good
As any road in Spain:
Men and maids can wander there, and Love's shaft
can strike
Just as deep a wound there as in the Athenian wood,
And shame to the poets who never found it out,
But it's true that the hills there are blue in the spring
And some folk are wed there with no gold ring.

Epithalamium, this, if you'll let it pass,
And I know for sure
That fine songs have been sung
For loves that wouldn't endure
As true for each other as these whose bed was grass
And no roof for cover, but only the pines that swung
Against high constellations, and Vega flashing fire
On the knitting of their two lives underneath the
     Lyre.

THEN, in Ohio, where it flattens out
From the blue hills the river sidles through,
Where the brown furrows lengthen in the fields,
They paused to reckon maps and mileages,
And dollars, for the Ford, insatiable,
Drank up both gas and oil beyond their fears.

In the long field beside the road a man
Stood leaning on a tractor, and the earth
Was drying on the furrow he had turned.
They heard him cough, a lean and sandy man,
And saw blood streaming sudden from his mouth;
He lurched, clutching the tractor, spun and fell.
John went to him. He could not speak, but signed
On, to the farm house at the hill edge. "Take,"
He gasped out, "Take me home." John carried him
Out to the car. In the field beyond, a team
Was dragging an old harrow, and their driver,
A Swede with bushy eyebrows, paused, and shot
A keen, cold glance at them, and slapped the reins
To start the team again. Before the house
A woman like some Teuton goddess stood

And waited. "Mag, I'm done," the man groaned out
As John laid him down, so weak and broken,
At her feet. "I knew you shouldn't work today."
"You never said so." She looked down the field.
"Ole can't run the thing." She turned to John.
"Want a job, Mister?" Children with pale hair
Came 'round the house and sat beside the man
On the green grass. "I wouldn't mind," said John.
"He's a mechanic. I must work the farm,"
The woman said. And John and April stayed.

John drove the tractor 'round and 'round the fields,
And the sun burned his face and arms to bronze;
Behind him, Ole harrowed, doggedly;
While April helped about the house, and fed
The hens, and washed the children's faces. Mag
Was always silent, and at table sat
Looking before her. Adolf too was still,
Lying upon a couch, and his face whitened,
All but the scarlet patches on his cheeks,
As John's took on its color. Ole spoke
But seldom, only to Mag, never in English.

"It's all experience," John said. "I get
Afraid," said April, evenings, in the swing

Beneath the maples. They put in the corn,
Checking the seed rows squarely, north and south
And east and west. . . . And then a midnight came
When Mag was knocking John and April's door.
"John, John," she called, "come help me. Adolf's
    worse."
John swung the door. She stood there with a candle,
Her nightgown buttoned underneath her chin.
"A moment," John said, slipping on his trousers.
He found Adolf in terror, breathing hard,
And bright blood down his nightshirt. Mag's eyes
    gleamed.
"I'll get the doctor," John said. "No, don't leave."
"April can go." "Do as you like," she said,
"Nothing does any good." But John called April,
And cranked up the Ford, and April started.
When John came back into the room, Mag sat
Leaned back against the wall at Adolf's head,
And now her gown was open, and her breasts,
Her great globed breasts, gleamed in the candle flare.
"This is the end of him," she said, and smiled,
A long, slow smile, and looked up in John's face.

The door swung open quietly, and Ole
Stood there, and gazed from under bushy brows.

"Get out," said Mag. But Ole shut the door
And stood against it, gazing sullenly.
Adolf's eyes were closed. "I hope to God I die,
But if I do, bring in the children first,"
Was all he said. Then Mag sat up, and wrapped
Her gown about her close. "Get out." The Swede
Shook his head once, said, "No," and so they waited.
John muttered softly, "I don't understand."
"I do," said Adolf, in a tired, thick voice.

The doctor came, and John and April went
Back to their bed. At morning, by the well,
Ole was waiting, and when John came out,
He spoke. "We got the corn in. Better now
You go." John said, "You're right." He cranked the
    Ford.
Mag paid him off. And April, looking back,
Saw in the doorway, standing, with still eyes,
Mag, like a goddess, waiting for some god.

You'll come to know the field
    When you've plowed it and seeded it;
You'll come to know love
    When you've utterly needed it.

28

And some men you get to know
By the tending of sheep;
And some nights you'll only learn
If you can't get your sleep.

There are folk you understand
By taking care of swine,
And some that only hunting wolves
Will give you the sign.

It's a grand world to learn about,
And its eating and its drinking,
But there's only a mite of it
You can sit and get by thinking.

ALONG the road they paused and reckoned up
And found they still had just the sum
That they had started with. "We're square," John said,
For stopping in Ohio . . . more than square."
Then they fell silent. They were more than square
For every farm along the road had come
To sound with voices, and no wall so blank
But through it they could feel the beat of blood
And the blind onset of some hidden longing;
No house was just a house, for a dim film
Of men and women struggling peopled it.
They spoke no more of Adolf, nor of Mag,
But both of them remembered, knowing well
That they had seen a bubbling in the spring
Of life, and smelled a fire-damp of dark Nature
And never would the pool again be still
Or look so shallow and so innocent.

April was driving when they came to town.
As they passed through, she stopped before a house

Where an old sign hung, dingy gold and black.
A woman sat on the porch. April went up
And spoke with her and came back to the car
With a faint light of pity in her eyes.
"Why did you stop?" She drove clear past the town
Before she answered:

                    "When I came last night,
She tried to send me on for someone else.
I said the need was too immediate.
She turned and said, 'He must decide it then.'
She did not want to let him go. His heart
Had given warning—has not strength to bear
These night alarms and rigors. 'What's this man,
This farmer, what's his failing spark to you
That you should go?' she said, protesting hard.
The doctor smiled, 'I must.' And then I knew.
He had so short a span of life before him—
So much to sweeten and enrich that span—
And yet he came. He wore death like a cloak
That muffled him against the night, and came.
For life to him, living beneath his doom,
Was infinitely precious, and no matter
Whose life it was, he must do all to save it.
I stopped and spoke to her. I had to know.
Last night, between here and the farm,

I saw a man . . . a man so great in pity,
So great in courage. . . . You had better drive.
I cannot see the road."

                    Her eyes brimmed over.

Brutus was pruning his orchard
   One day in the spring of the year
When Portia came out of the kitchen
   To fetch him a flagon of beer.
"It's good to be pruning the pear trees
   For all that Rome's falling, my dear."

Brutus, he set down the flagon
   And put on his toga again.
"I had almost forgotten it, Portia,
   But this is the Ides, and some men
Are waiting for me in the Senate.
   I must go—I must be there by ten."

And we know and he knew the ending
   But a Brutus must follow his bent;
And Portia was Cato's daughter
   She knew very well what he meant
And she took the beer back to the kitchen
   While he put on his toga and went.

* * *

At Philippi Brutus bethought him
  Of the pear trees, the flagon, and all,
And of Portia and how she knew better
  The day that he answered the call.

* * *

And the pear trees in Brutus's orchard
  Broke down with the fruit in the fall.

THE Wabash at old Vincennes bridge was up
And branches of green sycamores, and logs
And bits of roofs and corn-cribs floated by
Or dammed against the bridge-rails while the flood
Foamed over all the westward roads. That night
John backed the Ford into a tourist camp
Between a cabin and a yellow car
That had a tent slung from its top. A voice,
A rich Italian baritone, sang in the tent;
Between the showers, the singer cooked spaghetti
Over a fire in front. And in the tent
April had glimpses of a gold-haired girl
In a bright crimson-flowered kimono
Lounging upon a rumpled cot and smoking.
She was not singing, but from time to time
Her voice was raised, rebellious, querulous,
To curse the rain, and Tony, and her luck.
You get to know your neighbors in a camp:
Before the first night, they had Tony's heart
Laid open, and Elise's mystery.

"I want for have things fine. Now look this rain.
We have two weeks off, and I say to her,
You marry me—I take you for a trip
See Washington—that's Capitol, I say
It must be grand. And cherry blossom time—
I read about it. . . . You seen Washington?"

John said he had. "But you'll be late, won't you,
For cherry blossoms?"

                    "Mebbe so. Dam' rain.
She want go back to Cicero—and dance.
But I say big time—trip to Washington."

Elise's voice seared through the nuptial tent,
"Fer God's sake, Tony, get some cigarettes."

"Aw ri," and Tony splashed off down the camp.

The next day Tony hardly sang at all,
But once, when a brief burst of sudden sun
Shot through the clouds, he lifted up his voice.

"Fer God's sake, Tony, can the opera,"
And Tony's lips shut in a straight thin line.

"He wants to go to Washington," said April,
"And she to Cicero—to dance," John countered,
"And even if there were no flood, what then?"

But a grim silence settled on the tent
For the long afternoon of cold spring rain
That dimmed without a sunset into night.
Then through the night a scream of rage like fire:
"You God damned Wop, you take your damned blue
    chin
Offa my shoulder. Take your hands away.
I don't know why in hell I married you."
And then the screams were shut off as with fingers
Gripping the throat. Then blows that showered and
                                                   crashed
As the screams came again. And a long sob,
"I only want for take fine trip." "I'm through—
You understand—I'm through with lousy Wops!"

The tent became one whirlwind of blind blows.
The whole camp came astir. A siren screeched,
And a white glare of motorcycle lights
Lit up the wreck inside. Elise lay still
And Tony stood with pinioned arms and stared.
They took Elise upon a stretcher down
The rain-soaked road.

          "Jes' minute," Tony begged.
"Here, mister," and he turned to John,
"You tak' my tent. You pack my car for me.
I give you tent—you go for fine trip, west.
I go for jail ten days—she hospital.
I only want for fine trip too. No good.
So long."

        They led him off, and John and April
Acquired a tent that folded small and snug
And kept out water, when they patched up
Three dozen holes Elise's cigarettes
Had smouldered through the patent oilskin floor.

> *When you go southward*
>   *To meet the spring*
> *Look out for freshets*
>   *The south winds bring.*
>
> *When you go eastward*
>   *To greet the sun*
> *Keep an eye on your money*
>   *Or you'll have none.*
>
> *When you go northward*
>   *To find the snows*

37

Get in your firewood
   Before Autumn goes.

When you go westward
   To look for gold
Keep a stiff upper lip—
   It's scarce, I'm told.

When you stay too long
   In any one town
Beware of the earth-roots—
   They'll bind you down.

UNTIL you're past the close-fenced farms,
    until
You reach the open West and the great spaces,
You can't put up your tent along the road
Just anywhere, and take your ease in it.
Along the Sangamon, just southward from
The town where Lincoln first kept store, they camped
In Martin's pasture, near enough the house
So they could bring their water from his well.
Martin was willing, if they bought their milk
And eggs from him, though Martin had no name,
Locally, for his hospitality.
They might have searched the land of Egypt over
For a more crabbed household than was his,
But then, they could have found no lovelier pitch
To look out from than that beneath the oaks
The great white oaks, their leaves still flushed with
    rose,
On Martin's hilltop. On the sagging porch
It's weathered white paint scaling off, Old Pap
Sat in a hickory chair that rocked and squeaked.
Old Pap could see it all between the two

Gaunt hemlock trees that overhung the house—
The corn in squares, and parallelograms
Of winter wheat the color of robin's eggs.
Old Pap talked little, only sat and gazed,
Defeated and forgotten gentleness
In his pale eyes. He never said "my son,"
Or "George," when he would speak of Martin,
Who, coming in or going out, strode by
As if the old man were not there at all.

Beneath the oaks John worked for two whole days
To rehabilitate the wheezing Ford,
And evenings Martin came and stood
And watched with scornful and sardonic looks.
"The damn things are foolproof. She'll run, at that,"
Was all his word.
                    The two men lived alone
There in the house. A tousle-headed slut
Came up from the log shack below the hill
To cook for them. But Martin's barn was clean,
New-painted, and his horses sleek, his gear
For plowing, planting, harvesting, well oiled.
And April, sewing on the tent floor, shivered
At the gaunt hemlocks and the faded house
And the old man rocking his hickory chair.

It was so stark, so unapproachable,
So proof against impact of friendliness.
Yet looking down the fields to rounded hills
And blue woods westward, all was warm with spring.

The third day when the Ford's old engine came
As near in tune as you could ask of it,
April and John went over to the house
To get the milk and say goodbye at twilight.
Martin was on the steps. "Set down, set down,"
He said, and they obeyed him, wondering,
And April on a hopeful impulse spoke
Of the spread of beauty fading toward the west
And of their joy in it, and this and that,
Trying to make talk possible. Old Pap
Had ceased his rocking. Martin's voice went harsh.

"You been to college?"
                              "Yes, two years," said John.
"I was all set to go one time." Old Pap
Made a low clucking noise down in his throat.
"But I got cheated out of it. You see
That forty, down the road, I plowed today?
When I was seventeen, and huskier,
I reckon, than you ever was, that forty

Was unbroke bottom, stump land, and half swamp.
I was the youngest. Brothers gone away.
And my folks said, 'You clear that bottom forty
And you can have the crop and git some schoolin':
I took that land and stumped it, dreened it, broke it—
Two winters grubbin' in the frozen ground—
And put in corn. It was so rough I had
To hoe it hill by hill—no corn-plow'd make it.
And then I got a crop. There was a drought
That year, and the old fields, the prairie yonder,
Burned up. But my corn on the new broke bottom
Grew high and handsome, eared, and filled, and when
I started huskin', boy, I had the world
Tight by the tail. But Pap, he said, account
The drought, he'd have to have my crop, and took it.
And that's the last I ever spoke to him,
Nor him to me."

           The old man rose and stood
Shaking a little, looking down at Martin.
"I'm speakin' to ye now. Ye've gone too fur,
Ablabbin' it 'fore strangers this-a-way."
And he went slowly off toward the great barn.

"Where has he gone?" April asked brokenly.

"To hang himself. He's said he would, God knows
How many times."

                    But that time Old Pap meant it.

It's hardy folk that plant a hemlock tree
    Before the house.
For when it's young and you are young and free
It's fine to have it green beneath the snow
And hear it whisper to the winds that blow
    Across its boughs.

But when it's grown, if there be any hate
    Inside the door
Its fronds turn rusty; there's a kind of fate
That mutters in a hemlock, and you'll hear
The tree's tune change and a dry lisp of fear
    Will shake its core.

Beneath its bitter shade no flower will grow
    Nor glad green grass;
The sun comes through in ruddy coins that show
Upon the bare dry earth like fairy gold
And there's a smell of sun-forsaken mould
    When shadows pass.

When you are old, the ragged branches droop
  As tired as you;
Their arms grow lean and sapless; they will stoop
And feel with stringy fingers for some place
To rest their tattered trunks. They lack the grace
  To see life through.

But when you die, the hemlocks' requiem
  Is proud and brave.
Somehow they know the hour for you and them
And stand as though of life and all forsook
Like mourners vain that know how well they look
  Above a grave.

THE straight road runs well paved with farmers'
    votes
Criss-cross the thin-blazed trail George Rogers Clark
Broke through to take Vincennes—that wintry trail
His men had marked with bleeding feet to make
The wilderness Virginian. . . . And now
You can not see the trail. So long ago—
And not a ghost to whimper at the edge
Of frozen streams that barred their passage till
He plunged across, his red hair streaming wild
And dared his Long Knives follow. . . . Down these
    roads
The Ford careered in loud luxurious ease.

They made their camp at Chain of Rocks, and saw
Before them the gray waters from the North
Unmingled slide beside the silted stream
Mud-brown and swollen, flooding from the West.
They spread the tent, and from a corner crevice
They shook out a bright glint of gold—a ring
That rolled upon the patches of the floor,
And April picked it up. John came to see.

A ring, and inside it, engraved, the words:
"Forever. April . . . Nineteen thirty-one."
"We needed this," John said, and April smiled,
Turned grave, and questioned, "We don't know their
        name—
How can we send it back?" John shook his head.
"Elise won't want it. Tony doesn't know,
And if he did, what could he do with it?
They tried it once. It didn't work. For us
It will." She stood and held it in her hand
And looked back the long road that they had come.
"It may not be so simple. We can try."
John took it up and read the words aloud,
"Forever. April . . . Nineteen thirty-one.
Give me your hand. I meant to make one soon
From the first gold we get out of our mine.
With this ring I thee wed. I'm not afraid."
She kept it on, and kissed him, and they fell
To untangling the tent-ropes. But that night
She woke, and went outside, and looking up
Sought out bright Vega where the Lyre rode high
In the deep zenith; and she turned the ring
Slowly around her finger. "Not afraid,"
She whispered to herself. "I'm not afraid.
We'll make it work." She shivered and went back,

The circle with its pledge and its defeat
Upon her finger, crept in by John's side
And held him close until she went to sleep.

Easy roads to travel
Straight and smooth and white—
Scorn the dirt and gravel,
Speed by day or night.

Well the ways are charted
Open to your goal,
Bonds have all been marted
Never pay the toll.

Once the Sacs and Foxes
Made the war-trail here;
Where you truck your boxes
Hungry men stalked deer.

Bridges wide and open
Span the flooded creeks
Clark the bold Virginian
Waded to his breeks.

Progress, you may think it,
Now the way is clear

47

Fill your cup and drink it—
  Progress cost us dear.

Forget the empty flagons,
  Forget the men alone,
Forget the covered wagons,
  The convicts breaking stone.

Blood there was that bought it,
  Blood that couldn't rest.
We are ghosts that wrought it—
  The highway to the West.

THE man Tobias stood and laughed alone
And looked down on the river and the lands
New rising as the flood went down, and splashed
With bright pools of reflected sunset sky;
And so they found him when they stopped to ask
If they might set their tent up in his orchard.
"Yes, if ye ain't afeared," he said, and laughed
Again, still looking out across the flats.
"Afeared of what?" John asked him, wondering.
"Afeared o' me, and of the widder's curse.
She's comin' yender. Set and hear," he said.
Far down below, across the bright-pooled mud
A boat was making for the shore. "The river's
    shifted."
Again he laughed, full-throated, as the boat
Was hauled up on the bank. And then they watched
A woman pick her way amidst the pools
Sky colored, in the ancient river bed
And come, tall and bedraggled, up the slope.

She faced the man Tobias for a space.
"You'll claim on this?" she said.

      "Don't have to claim.
It was an act of God. The law says so.
I always said there warn't no God, but now
It looks ongrateful. I'm an atheist,
I always said, and you was feared of me
Because I said it. Well, your man was drowned.
You said God took him. You looked down on me.
God gives me half a section of good land
And leaves you just a strip of rocky pasture
For all your prayers and piety." No laughter now.

"But God can turn the river back again."

"He won't do that."
      "So you acknowledge Him."

"Not yet, unless I must to get the land."

"It was your fishing pier that started it,"
She said accusingly. "If there's a law,
It must take some account of that."

      "Guess not.
God and the old Missouri take no 'count
Of where I build a fishin' pier. The law
Is on my side. And I'd be thanking God
If I could find him, for your farm, my dear."

The twilight air went sudden very still.
The woman stood and looked at him, and seemed
Somehow to have no anger in her eyes—
No more reproach. "If you could just find Him,"
She said at last, and turned to go. The man
Tobias stopped her.

                    "There's one way, you know,
For you to get it back." She bent her head
Slowly, and slowly moved down the steep path.
The man called after, "Rachel, wait." She stopped.
"I'll row you over. She's still mighty swift."
The woman waited, looking back at him.
He turned to John. "You never mind your tent.
Go in the house and rustle up your supper.
I can't afford to turn no one away
Tonight. The ground's wet. Make yourselves to
    home.
I always said I was onlucky. Now,
I ain't so sure." He strode off down the path.

April went in and raked the kitchen coals
And set the lonely table for themselves
And for one more: perhaps their host would come.
But three hours later, when the man Tobias
Came back again, he was too drunk with joy

(Or else with Rachel's former husband's rum)
To eat or sleep or be an atheist.

The high stars wheel in their courses;
   You may map them and measure them true,
You may calculate distances, forces—
   But that's about all you can do.

The mountains that rose in the morning
   Of earth, you may wonder and climb,
But if you would move them, take warning
   You can't—you must leave them to Time.

The great river flows as it pleases;
   You may sail it, or swim it, or stay
Where you are on the bank till it freezes
   But you never can make it obey.

The heart when it quickens and quivers
   Is a peril no life is above,
And the stars and the mountains and rivers
   Are as easy to manage as love.

A GAY smile and a twisted foot are worth
No end of thumbs and curses by the road—
You simply can not pass a man like that
For all the front seat of a Model T
Is built for two. They picked up such a man
And found him rich in wisdom of the land,
Its guide and fabulist. He seemed to have
No hard fixed destination, but to serve
Their inclinations with his knowledges.
On his suggestion—he gave no advice—
They turned to southward, to the Ozark Mountains,
For the long road had been a monotone
Through the flat mileages of wind-blown corn
That ran to flat horizons and they longed
For the blue lift of hills. And as they drove
The smiling man who had the twisted foot
Talked wonders, while they watched for jagged peaks
To rise against the sun. Hills folded in,
There were no peaks, no blue immensities,
But round hills, gentle, forested, and calm.
The day was hot, and John took off his coat.
The Ford was thirsty at the long ascent,

And every stream they passed they dipped and filled
    it.
No farm lands stretched beside this trail
But cabins in the clearings, hides nailed up
To dry, and men with dogs and guns,
Lean men, and women shy, in calico,
Who seemed forever fetching wood and water.

"This road," the genial passenger explained,
"Will take us to Big Spring. You'll see it soon—
The biggest water spring in all the world.
It feeds a river, by itself alone.
And you can camp there—none'll chase you off."

The sun went down before they came to it,
But gazing at it, John and April felt
The day well spent that brought them. From the
    foot
Of a steep hill they saw the spring gush out
And tumble foaming into a great pool
Whose farthest edges trembled with the surge
That brimmed it over, and a river took
Its source from this one pool. The shadows fell
And chilled them as they marvelled. John turned back
To get his coat. His coat was gone. And there,

Where he had thrown it was another coat,
A ragged coat, with empty pockets. "Where
In hell?" —He looked around. The passenger
Was also gone. They had not seen him go
As up the steep blind trail across the hill
He strode, unsmiling, with no twisted foot.

I met Autolycus one sunny day
When I was riding through the Ozark Mountains.
I found him very pleasant company,
His songs were new and most uncommon gay;
He levelled mountains and he gathered hours
Into a nosegay of diverting flowers;
We ate together, from my scrip of course,
And drank from half a dozen wayside fountains.
His tales were no end moral: righteously
He told how he had once met Jesse James
But when he found out who the man might be
He disapproved of him. He praised my horse
And laughed at all the gems of my discourse.

We bivouacked snug that night beside a fountain.
Next morning when I woke I found him gone
And that he'd left his shirt and taken mine.
I'd go agunning for Autolycus

But that the pocket where I had my gun
Was in a pair of breeches he had on.
Some poets make him out a jolly cuss.
I disagree with them. . . . He took my horse.
The rascal has no head for mine and thine,
No sense of obligation, no remorse.
He's just a hobo on some Ozark Mountain.
It's true he's full of songs and curious games
And lofty talk of human parity,
But I don't rate him innocent, for one;
A verdict should be struck with clarity:
I stand for justice, human or divine:
He stole my horse, my breeches and my gun,
And worse than this, for all his talk was fine,
The bastard spilled my Christian charity.

APRIL could eat no breakfast the next day
And hardly noticed it. She had to rip
The pocket she had sewn into her dress
To get the folded crisp ten dollar bill
She kept there for emergencies like this
Along with the certificate with doves
And roses they had got in West Virginia.
That day they did a deal of counting up.
This dimmed the prospect. . . . Who'd have thought
    a man
With such a smile and such a flow of cheer
Would prove a thief? For in John's vanished coat
Was what was left of their Ohio stake
And more the man Tobias paid them when
They left him. They had stayed a month
To help him rush a crop into the flats
The river gave him. John had engineered
A rip-rap dike—"lest God should change His mind,"
Tobias put it—'cross the old stream bed;
And John had worked with axe among the willows,
And an old tractor that Tobias borrowed,

To make new lands safe. And while he worked
Along his dike, Tobias, with his mules
And Rachel's, plowed the slowly drying field.
Tobias paid them well, and they had left
The day Tobias had brought Rachel home.
April had trimmed the house for her, and shed
Some tears about it, for no reason. Now
All they had earned was gone, and John was wearing
A ragged coat that might at any time
Be recognized for highway larceny.
"We'd best get out of this." "We won't get far."
They turned northwestward, leaving the round hills,
And when the sun began to burn, John hung
The coat upon a fence-post, and drove on.
April was pale. The mountain curves, she said,
Made her a little car-sick. It would pass.
They had no lunch that day, and when at night
A farmer's wife provided chicken dinners
"In Southern style, with fixin's, for four bits,"
She and her hunger still were fighting hard.
John's face was troubled, but the farmer's wife
Smiled shrewdly, came and patted April's cheek
And said, "It's only natural. Don't cry.
But do your best—you have to eat for two."

They drove on from the farm a dozen miles,
Talking by spurts in a forced gayety,
And found a camp site. When the tent was up
And blankets spread, a silence fell on them.
John could not jest again about the man
Who seemed to have the twisted foot. The jests
Were dry. They faced it now. He had no coat.
They'd broken their last ten. The farmer's wife? . . .
John's thoughts went racing out ahead of them.
He could not ask his question. April sat
And traced the leafy pattern of the shadows
The trees against the moon cast on the tent.
"She may be right," she said at last. "And if——"
"It's plain," John said, "that I must get a job."
"Don't worry, dearest." April's smile was wan.
He could not tell, by moonlight, in the tent,
Whether her eyes had fear in them or joy,
But he could see she smiled. That night they slept
With her head on his shoulder, not as always
Till then, with his on hers. The morning sun
Etched the leaf patterns clear, and when he woke
Her eyes were open, tracing them again.

Lead out your dreams
  And let your reveries run,

Youth, for the hour will come too soon
When Life will bridle all beneath the moon
  And you will find your dreaming day is done.

Dance while you can
  And Time will pay the piper,
Lad, but you never can be sure
When he will change his tune, and your
  Slim legs will stiffen when your judgment's riper.

Ride a high horse
  And flaunt while flaunt you may,
Lass, and put on your scarlet gown—
There'll come a night when you must wear your
    brown
  And old regrets make passing mean array.

Plant with the spring
  And let your plow sink deep,
Man, for who knows how early frost
May fall upon the grain and all be lost?
  Plant—and be ready when it's time to reap.

THEY worked on westward, asking as they
   went
At farms and filling-stations, for a job.
No luck. "The things I should have learned," John
   found,
"Are how to milk, and how to drive a mule.
Let's head for Kansas—they use tractors there."
Just out from Independence, they drew up
Before a camp with rustic cottages
And a red sign that told the passing world
This was the spot where the great wagon trains
Outfitted for the trail to Santa Fe
A hundred years ago. John spoke his piece.
The lad beside the gas pumps cut him off.
"Don't need nobody." Then a kind of smile,
And, "Might try Ed's place. It's just down the road,
And Ed, he let his helper go last week."
John thanked him and drove on. Ed's Place—
Four slab-side cabins and a barbecue.
Ed stood beside the pumps, a stubbly man,
And when John asked for oil, he struck his note
Facetiously, with a grim kind of gag:

"What flavor, Mister?" "Pennsylvania."
"Okay." And Ed brought out a battered quart
In an old copper cup. John knew the Ford
Was most fastidious, but he did not know
The source of Ed's supply, or that Ed's pumps,
Whatever they were labeled, all were filled
With just one product. But the price was less
And Ed's big sign proclaimed the gas he sold
Was cheap—two cents below the common rate.
John asked his question. Ed spat, thoughtfully.
"I might," he said. "Yes, I might take you on.
"Hard up?" "Flat broke." "Okay. I'll tell you what.
I'll give you house room in a cabin here
And chuck, for both, there from the barbecue."
"I've got a tent," John said. "Don't need the cabin."
"That's better yet. You take the pumps from six—
The farmers come in early—until four,
And I'll allow you ten a week. And chuck.
I'll take the night shift. I been short a hand.
But you must mind your business." John agreed,
And drove in at the far end of the lot,
Beyond the cabins, and set up the tent.
Ed gave him his instructions. "There's two kinds,
There's red and regular. If they want to know
What brand we keep, it's Independent, see.

And two cents cheaper. And that's all. Get goin'."
A car drove up. John filled it and then sprang
With the alacrity of one on trial
To clean the wind-shield. Ed watched sullenly,
And when the car drove on, he said, "You'll do.
But don't be washin' wind-shields, 'less they ask.
I don't put on no airs, and I don't want none."
At six each day John stood to man the pumps
And they were always full, although he saw
No trucks drive up to fill them. Ed took over
Each day at four. "You'd better keep your wife
Close in the tent," he said the second day,
"Specially evenings—this crowd's pretty rough."
Saturday came. That night the farther cabin
Was rented out three times, and April's sleep
Was broken by the shrill and drunken laughter
As couples came and went. On Sunday morning
John filled a car for one with bleary eyes,
And counted change into a hand that shook.
The man's car reeled along the road. John watched,
And when it disappeared, found at his feet
Six dollars of the change. The man was gone.
John made a mental note to watch for him
And put the money in his pocket. Sunday night
Again their sleep was shattered. Uniforms

Of state police were all about the place
And one of them called sternly at the tent.
John came out blinking. Two men in plain clothes
Were holding Ed. An oil truck without lights,
Its Texas license plates bedaubed with mud,
Was standing by the pumps. Ed looked at John
And spat. "You whelp—I should 'a' knowed,
When I see where your lousy car was from,
You was a dick." "Shut up." A keen-eyed man,
Who seemed to have authority, commanded.
"I've got all I want. These here nests are yours."
The cabins were all routed out and cleared
By town police, and April ripped again
The sewed-up pocket, and brought out her lines
To prove respectability. The squad
Made off, with Ed and two men from the truck,
And certain angry and dishevelled couples,
Leaving the gas pumps all officially
Sealed up with paper. John turned off the lights,
Went back to sleep, and when the morning came
They found the frightened Negro cook alone
In the deserted barbecue. "Mist' John,"
She whimpered, "I'll get you all's breakfast.
And then, ef I was you, I'd move along."
"What was it all about?" asked April.

"I don' know nothin'. Seems like Mister Ed
Ain't gone paid taxes on 'at bootleg gas.
Las' time they took him thirty days. This time,
Mos' like, they'll send him up to Leavenworth.
Them G-men, they don't fool. You better go."

We're told, "If we take the devil's pay
   We must do the devil's work."
But why should the devil have the say?—
   He taught us how to shirk.

Why should you give the devil his due?
   Life doesn't pay her debts—
And what has the devil done for you?
   He's coppered all his bets.

These proverbs guide and rule the race,
   And half of them are lies
"You can't touch pitch" and stay in grace—
   But every sailor tries.

And it's the Motive—not the Deed,
   The Irish poet sings
And the Light of Lights will intercede
   To settle who rates wings.

So take your fortune up, my lad
  And shake your legs and revel—
The chances may not be so bad
  That you'll have to pay the devil.

THERE was a farm near Lawrence where they
    worked
A week. The household had a son who fixed
Blue amorous eyes on April. They moved on.
Then near Topeka where they stopped a while
The farmer's sister took to following
John to the wheat field—and they moved again.
A census bureau phrase ran through their heads.
"We're 'casual labor,'" John said soberly,
"We know the tables—seasonal employment—
And how it rates in economic scales,
But what else is there? We must see it through."
The wheat fields burned. His eyes were red with dust.
There was one comfort: no one had a coat.
Then for a month they joined a threshing outfit
Where John earned more, and sometimes April too
Would take her turn beside the kitchen stove
And help the women with the threshers' dinners
And after sundown help to wash the dishes.
John got three dollars, April only one.
For by that summer farmers never knew
How soon the farms would follow down the banks

Into some ruin no one understood.

"There's wheat enough," John said, "and wheat is
    food."

"The car won't run on wheat. We'll get through
    Kansas

But who would think a state could be so long?"

"We'll get through somehow. When the wheat's all in

What do we do?" "I wish you wouldn't look

Nine months ahead as if the world would end

Some night next spring. I'll be all right." She smiled.

"You'll do your part. I'm not so sure of mine,"

John muttered, thinking of the talk

That ran among the threshing crew—the talk

Of men who never in their lives had looked

Ahead to years like this—all promise blank—

And only planned for some escape to states

Where they could get themselves too drunk to think.

"We might go back," John thought. . . . She read his
    thought.

"To what?" . . . "Your aunt in Washington—she
    might——"

"Not on her pension." . . . April's eyes were calm

And he read something from the way she sat

Facing the sunset. . . . But no word of this

Was ever spoken out, aloud, between them.

The last high load of golden sheaves came up.
The thresher boss paid off the crew, hooked up
His caravan and trundled northward. John
And April loaded up their tent and turned
West on the road a hundred years ago
Those bolder caravans had followed through
To find their desert fortunes. Where they watched
For trace of buffalo or Indian signs,
John scanned the dumps for wreckage of old Fords
That he might pillage for spare parts. The gasket
Had given out and every puff of power
Came through with a sharp gasp of pain.
And Number One, the bearing of most risk
In the old Model T, was ripe to go;
And any wayside junk pile might give up
A gasket and a bearing Number One
If you had strength and patience to extract it.
Two days, and fifty slow and sunburnt miles
And hours of struggle with enrusted bolts
Yielded the parts. They stopped beneath a maple
That had a strong branch level over them,
And sweated off the head block. April swung
Her weight upon a piece of braided fence-wire,
Thrown pully-wise across the limb above,
To lift the block, and John put in the gasket.

And with what tools they had, in two more days
They got the bearing in. It too was worn
But served. They scrubbed their hard, grease-black-
    ened hands
With sand in a warm pool—all that was left
Of water in a little river channel.
They took their hour to rest. Harvest was in:
They had their portion: they had put their gear
In order for new marches: all was well. . . .
But something of the future had gone dim
To John: what if those men were right? He knew
They had no grasp of things, no marshalling
Of the great ebb and flow of gold and time,
No prophet-craft—and yet—their eyes were dull
Looking ahead. Their instincts had gone cold.
And John's thin slogan-braced collegiate creed
Was wearing through. What if those men were right?
The soft warm twilight died away. The sky
Was great with more stars than they'd ever known:
Too many stars. John lay upon his back
And looked up, but he had no heart to trace
Familiar constellations. April sat
As quiet as the prairie and the night
And looked and looked at Venus going down

Bright in the west. Her instincts were unblurred.
She knew. Those days she always faced the west.

Horace Greeley told my father
   To "Go West, Young Man, go West"
And my father took his counsel
   Thinking Horace must know best.

And my father took the ague
   Like a foolish pioneer
And my mother had to nurse him
   And nurse me, poor patient dear.

Horace Greeley sat and thundered
   Bolt on bolt he forged and hurled
From the office of the Tribune
   Down upon the stupid world.

While the 'hoppers ate the corn crop
   And the rust devoured the wheat
And the drought killed off the cattle
   (And the in-ter-est to meet!)

But old Horace seldom wandered
   From his sanctum and his beer

And who says he wasn't wiser
  Than some docile pioneer?

But if father hadn't heeded
  What old Horace had to say
And gone out to take the ague
  What would Kansas (or Wisconsin
Illinois or Ioway
  Or Missouri or Nebraska or Dakota) be today?

PAST Newton, upon every roll of prairie
In spindling pyramids, oil derricks stood
Against the sky. A side road there led off
"To GUSHER—Future Oil Metropolis,"
And a still louder sign-board marked the way
"To SIMON ROCKETT'S BLACK GOLD EL
    DORADO."
The road was rutted deep by many trucks.
John took it: here there must be work. That day
On Simon Rockett's tract, the time-keeper
Was drunk, and so John got his job.
The "future city" was two rows of shacks
Beside the rutted road. And not one tree
To break the wind that seemed about to blow
The tent away. Two restaurants, the Greek's,
And Sari's New Hungarian Cafe
Stood cheek by jowl to feed the swarming crews
Of hungry drillers from the Continent Oil
And Simon Rockett's lot. It was a race,
Since the two rival leases lay so close,
To see who first would reap and waste the field.
The Continent people worked efficiently

With keen geologists to watch the cores
Of each drill's cutting. But the other crew
Was of a different stripe. They called themselves
The wild cats—and they proved it, too. Each day
Came Simon Rockett in his Cadillac
To boss his drillers. Simon was a man
Who said his thumb could analyze a crude
Better than any chemist. . . . But he washed
His thumb and put on gloves before he sold
The stock certificates in El Dorado.
He tramped the field in high-laced yellow boots,
Twirled his mustache, and called upon his God,
To verify his least asseveration.
He was an oil man, Yes sirree, by God,
And he swore El Dorado would be good
For twenty million barrels. He knew. No need
For these geologists—they only guessed
And he guessed better—Yes siree by God. . . .
Yet no one knew how he acquired the lease.
Well Three was yielding; and at One and Two
He kept the pump beams rocking, though no oil
Came up their tubings. And when Number Four
With a great crash came in, it proved a gasser,
And Simon stood to windward, threw a match

To set it off, and let the flames roar up
To light the sky, and Gusher, for three nights
Before its blast went down. In Hutchinson
He pasted on his gleaming office window
The cubage of Dorado's latest strike
In liberal estimate. It might sell stock.
He had no time for gas—he drilled for oil.
He loved the oil-smell. Gas was just a stink.

John earned his money there on Rockett's lease
And April worked in Sari's New Cafe
For Sari's gnarled hands could not keep it up
For all her peasant tirelessness. Each month
Old Sari went to town and lettered out
An unpronounceable old world address
And sent her profits off—to Hungary.
The winds turned bitter cold. April and John
Moved into Sari's shack and took the room
She'd used for wine—for she had made a vintage
From grape-bricks, sugar and odd lots of fruit,
That gave her tavern popularity
Until the law came down and shut it off.
With winter, and the falling price of crude,
The Continent Oil crowd lifted out their drills

And half the men in Gusher left. The Greeks
Gave up the battle. For a little while
Sari was prosperous. The winter seemed
To give old Simon Rockett higher spirits.
His stock was selling, though no wells came in,
And even Number Three was slowing down.
Then, on a pay-day, something went amiss.
There was a system in old Simon's pay-days:
He came with a great roll of bills and peeled
The wages for each driller off from it;
He seemed to keep no books, beyond John's time-
    sheet.
But this day, Simon didn't come at all.
The men showed no surprise. Wild catter's trick.
They telephoned to Hutchinson. No sign
Of Simon Rockett. No one answered there.
They crowded into El Dorado's trucks
And drove to town, and tore the iron fence
From Rockett's lawn, swarmed in, and broke
His windows, systematically, fought
Ten minutes with police and deputies,
And vanished, tools and trucks and all,
While John and April sat in Sari's kitchen
And waited, vainly, for a customer.

That night two feet of snow came down. The roads
Were blocked. The weeks went by. The coal gave
    out.
They burned the fences, then a shack or two,
And lived on Sari's stock of canned goods, bought
With credit while the Gusher boom was on,
And some spare hams and bacon she had hung
In the back shed. . . . April was heavy now
And Sari did the housework, while each day
They scanned the sky for sign of winter's breaking.
The first thaw came. The snow fields patched and
    bare,
The derricks black. The road a stream of mud.
And at the door, first sign of spring—the sheriff.

John stood him off with half the cash he had.
He'd come again, he said, and Sari might,
Unless she had some good collateral,
Go with him to the County Farm. Next week.
"I'll go," said Sari, "if they'll let me cook.
It's not so bad. I been on county farms
Before. But you—you better take her out
Of this. This is no place for have a kid."
April came over and kissed Sari's eyes—

So old and wrinkled and so undismayed.
Next week the sheriff came, and Sari went.

A million years, the slogans say
  Dame Nature took to brew
In secret sands her deodands
And trillions of fat and spongy creatures
With scaly cadavers and vacant features
  Died to carry her recipe through.

And we hurl ourselves through the stratosphere
  And we hit the road at eighty
And we speed and slay on the State's highway
And financier and piano-tuner
Die to get there a moment sooner
  As though the matter were really weighty.

And we must strike oil or we can't have gas,
  Till we find some other scheme,
So we drive and drill and we pump and spill
And millions of years we waste in a minute
And still we shout—There are millions in it. . . .
  But who knows where the black oil flows
  Till Fortune tips the beam?

THE roads in Kansas all looked just alike—
No land-mark—nothing they could quite remember—
Until they came to one that ran for miles
Along beneath a limestone outcrop wall;
Then, winding upward, slowly winding upward,
A grade they hardly noticed, to a crest,
A sudden crest, and there, another land.
The road fell sharp below them, and the world
Changed in an eye-wink. . . . They remembered
    this:
All treeless, fenceless, boundless to the rim
Of a horizon level as taut wire,
And farther off, beneath a farther blue
Than any eastern and hill-fettered eye
Could sweep to. Here the road ran straight.
And here the mind shook off its last record
Of sheltering elms and fireside certainties,
And motion was a drift of tumble-weed
The long winds captained, and the whirls of dust
That rose and spun and scattered like blown cloud.
The miles slid under them. They lifted voice
And sang above the rattling of the Ford.

Long miles. And nothing—but the open world.
Lean cattle, tiny in the distance, stood
In false ponds of the plains mirage, their legs
Seeming to disappear in glimmering lakes;
And a far ranch-house, riding in the sky
As if it stood in some mysterious sea
Of cloud, or wave, or propped on stilts above
A sea-blue water with no farther shore.
They sang through all the songs they knew,
And started over. All day long they sang.
Sometimes the road led on beside the bank
Of a slow river, wide and wandering
In convolutions through the sandy bars
That almost choked its flat and crawling bed
With dry and drifting islands. By the river
A few old cottonwoods stood up and waved
Beneath the never slackening wind. And when
The sun was just about to cut, blood red,
Into the sharp horizon, they first glimpsed
A blur of smoke—Dodge City—and the end
Of the old Chisholm Trail, and long ago
The rail head—for a time a place of wrath
And glory, in frontier mythology.
To John and April, Dodge was just a place

To end a day they never could forget—
An end of sunshine and of singing miles.
For the next morning, everything went strange,
And hung with fate. . . . That day they did not sing.

I met a man who knew Wild Bill
  And Two Gun Smith, he said
And he had drunk with Masterson
  The day they shot him dead:
O now, I thought, I'll get the truth
  Straight from the fountain head.

O let me shake the hand that shook
  The hand of Masterson
And tell me just how Wild Bill looked
  And how he fanned his gun
To shoot six cattle thieves at once
  Before the skunks could run.

O tell me, man who lived in Dodge
  With those great heroes then,
Were they as swift and cool and brave
  In life as history's pen
Has made them out. Those marshals all
  Were estimable men.

Hold on, he said, you got me wrong
  Get this before you shake
For my best friend met up with them
  And never got a break,
And he was all the friend I had—
  They shot him by mistake.

He wiped his eye and took a drink
  As if he drank alone.
He was the only friend I had—
  He come from San Antone. . . .
And the man who knew Bat Masterson
  Sat still as any stone.

I'm sorry now I met the man
  Who knew the marshals well
Research is so confusing to
  A scribe who wants to sell
The glorious legends of the West
  And finds 'em false as hell.

THE night they slept at Dodge the wind veered
  south
And the high air was clouded, with no clouds
Of any rain beneficent, but dust
As if the top soil of the Panhandle
Had been caught up and sifted into it.
At first they drove on, wondering, not afraid
But only curious. They had read of this.
Their luck was with them—they would see it now.
The dust closed down. The passing cars burned lights
As if the night had fallen; and the sun
Above them turned a steel-blue disc that hung
In coffee-colored air, and then went out.
Mid-afternoon they had to leave the car
To read the sign that told them they had passed
Through Kansas, at the Colorado line.
A few miles farther, and they found the road
Had vanished in a waste of swirling mud.
The concrete had washed out. There was no sense
Or reason in it. All the world was dust—
Thick choking dust—and here a flood. Some tracks

Swung northward—an unmarked detour. They fol-
lowed.
The tracks at first were plain. Then, suddenly,
They too were lost upon a wind-swept ridge.
John set the Ford in a wide circle till
He found a track. It might have been his own—
He could not tell. If so they would get back
To the last ghostly town they had come through.
If not, it must lead somewhere. Now and then
The tires would chatter through a drift of sand
That wiped the tracks out. Once in such a drift
The Ford stalled dead. And April sat and counted
Three times, to ninety. . . . At the third, her face
Twitched at a sharper pain. . . . "My time has come,"
She said, and, "Don't be frightened. It's just natural.
But not . . . convenient. We had best turn back."
So John got out. She took the wheel. He pushed
Against the boiling radiator frame.
They cleared the drift. He spun the car about
And gave it gas. "There won't be time," she said.
He set his teeth. The track was lost again,
And there beside them, looming in the dust,
A rancher's hut—the doorway blocked with sand.
John broke it open. The deserted house
Was almost empty, but there was a bunk

Where John threw in the blankets and laid April.
"It's not so far back to that town," she said.
"You'd better go for help. I'll be all right."
"No . . . I won't leave you." "Yes, you will. This is
My party. Kiss me and go quick. It may
Be morning by the time it comes." John tried
To shut the door. "No. Leave it open. Please.
You've three hours more of daylight. It's not far."
John turned the Ford and started. "Can't be far,"
He muttered, saying it again, over
And over to himself. The track was fresh.
He had three hours. . . . It can't be far. . . . Five miles
He followed it. Then in a drift, the Ford
Stuck fast. He twitched and backed. . . . The wheel
Spun in his hand and the thick air went black
As his head fell against the useless wheel.
He struggled up, and dug the compass out
From the camp litter in the back. He knew
The town lay to southeastward. As he ran
He lost the track. He paused, and circled, found
Another. Then he stopped. "Now steady on,"
He said aloud. He set the compass down
And leveled it upon a heap of sand.
And from the gloom a sudden glare of lights
Struck sidelong. He could barely leap aside

As a long car came through and ground the compass
Into its rut. John shouted, but the car
Went on. They had not seen or heard. But John
In its flash past had caught a kind of glimpse
Of a red cross above the license plate,
And John ran shouting, sobbing, after it.

And April counted, counted, in the bunk.
The pains came faster. April's mind was clear.
She threw the blankets off, and laid herself
On the old corn-husk mattress of the bunk.
She found two corn cobs in the corner of it
And gripped them hard. At first she met the pains
With her lips set. But as they tore her through,
More imminent, she shouted at each pain
And thought of . . . cheering at a football game.
"No use to be too lady-like," she said
Between two travail throes, "there's no one here
To know if I keep still." The daylight left
The open doorway. . . . One bone-wrenching pain.
A pause. A moment. Then the final burst
Of agony and all her strength went forth
In answer to it. And she knew 'twas done.
She waited. . . . No cry came. None ever came.
And in the great assuagement, April wept.

Past midnight, and the Doctor's headlights flared
Through the half-open door, and a faint voice
From April greeted them: "Hello. Come in."
John leaped out, but the Doctor barred his way.
"Get me the water can—left running-board—
The water, mind you, not the oil or gas—
And see if there's a stove." John found the can
And brought it in. The Doctor had his flash-light
Hung in the bunk, and by the beam of it
Was working over April. "Where's the child?"
John choked out. April did not speak.
"It's not alive," the Doctor said at last.
John sank against the door. "Too late." The Doctor
Turned, said, "No. It would have made no diff'rence.
Start a fire," and went back to his work.
There was no stove, and John went out and gathered
Some branches from an old dead tamarisk
And got the water heating. When he came
Back in the house, a tiny bundle lay
Wrapped in a crackling, yellowed *Denver Post*
Beside the bunk. And April spoke. "John dear,
Go dig a grave. And dearest, please don't look."
John went, and with his hands and a sharp stick
Hollowed a place beneath the tamarisk
Where there was a reflected headlight glow.

John took the bundle, tenderly, this clot
Of both their bloods, still-born and born too soon,
Into the dusty night, and buried it.
The Doctor said, "Now steady, Missus; we
Have got to get this done before we go,
And it will hurt." And April: "I don't mind."
When John returned, the Doctor said, "You might
Have used my spade, there on the running-board.
Forgot to tell you." And he washed his hands
Again. There was no water left for John's.
The Doctor's face was grave. "A hospital?"
"Not one in fifty miles. I'll find some place."
They lifted April, set her in the car.
The Doctor gave John orders: "Hold her steady.
She mustn't bleed too much. And keep the blankets
Around her close. The wind's turned north. I'll drive,
And take it slow." And April in John's arms
Lay quiet, only murmuring now and then,
Trying to give him cheer. The night was cold
And the dust breaking. Some faint stars came out.
Before they reached the town, the night was gone.

And two days after, when John found his car
And brought a steering knuckle, second-hand,
To mend it with, he found some one had slept

In it. The tent was rumpled on the floor
For some one's bivouac, some one who had smoked
Two packs of Lucky Strikes, and thrown the butts
Out on the sand drift. John made inventory.
Nothing was missing but one book of verse.
('Twas Edna Millay's *Fatal Interview*.)
And on the seat a note, in pencil, scrawled
Upon a fly-leaf torn from it: "I need
This book. Thanks for the buggy ride."

> *Houses of cards*
> *And Castles in Spain:*
> *Fate interlards*
> *The grief with the gain:*
> *Babe in the womb*
> *And seed in the ground—*
> *Life to the tomb*
> *And castles to shards.*
> *On the way to Spain*
> *Are tall ships drowned,*
> *And the seed needs rain,*
> *Yet we stack the cards*
> *The wind blows down,*
> *And we dream the towers*
> *That fall to shards.*

And what of the hours
We build and plan—
Are they not the crown
Of the days of man?
For Hope still guards
From Fate and pain
Our houses of cards
And Castles in Spain.

BEYOND Las Animas—and John found work.
There dry and tawny lands were being plowed,
And Mexicans were scarce, and melon seeds
Must be put in that very moon, or lose
The early market; all the country round
Would be one melon patch by June; a man
Who could sort seeds, and plant, and drive a tractor
Was worth his salt—with some salt for his wife;
And when the seeds were in, someone must splash
About the sluice-gates, letting in the water.

Before the ranch-house, April, in the sun
Took color into her plae cheeks, although
The dust still hung above them, and the day
Came whitely through. The days were very good
But the long nights were haunted. April knew
By sunlight, in the healing of the wind,
That a great storm had passed, and was content.
But in the night, a shadow tugged at her
And would not let her sleep. There was a row
Of tamarisks by the ranch-house, and she sat
And counted them, serenely, afternoons,

But when dusk fell, she could not look at them.
At last she wakened John. "There's something wrong
With me," she said. "I don't know what it is.
A sort of complex—like Antigone.
Could we go back—just for a day—go back
To . . . to the place you buried him?" Till then
John never knew she knew it was a boy.
He had not looked. And now that clot of both
Their bloods was calling her. "We'd never find
The place," he answered, knowing in his heart
It was not good for her to yearn for it,
But having quick to tongue no argument
To clear her fantasy, no word that seemed
Neither too hard nor too unkind. "The house,"
She answered, "must lie off the road, to northward.
A withered tamarisk—the doctor knows
The way. We could ask him. And I must go.
Just for an hour. You know I never wanted
Before, to turn back. Now——" Her whisper broke.
An inward moan went through John's weary frame,
A wave of something like remorse, a beating
Of tortured love. To him the tamarisks
Had spoken too, but he had set himself
To look at them and look away again
With no compulsive tears behind his eyes.

"Well, if you like, we'll go. But dearest, dearest——"
"When?" "Tomorrow." April's head sank back
And in a moment she was fast asleep.

When morning came, the dust-red upper air
Was blue and crystal. April came refreshed
Out in the sun, looked at the tamarisks
As one who faced a world not too malign
To be endured. They would go back. . . . And then
She looked to westward. There the Spanish Peaks,
Two gleaming drifts of snow against the sky,
The north a cone, the south a camel-back,
Hung beckoning. Two mountains. Far away.
First they had seen. John came to her, and "Wait,"
She said, and "Look. Leave me alone." John went
Without a word back to the house. She sat
And traced the snow-clad masses with her eyes.
An hour went by. And something she had had
Deep in her being long and long before
Came near and nearer: she went back in time
And space and sense of some strange immanence.
The hut by the dead tamarisk, till then
A half-seen thing that drew and tortured her,
Let go its hold. She lost it, and no will
Was left in her to go and seek it out.

When John came back, he found her facing west
Again, her gaze upon the Spanish Peaks,
Untroubled. "I have changed my mind," she said.
"We're free. There's no good now in turning back."
The wind was waving the slim tamarisks
And April stood and waved her arms with theirs.

When Duse said to Isadora
    Soulfully, "Gardez la grande douleur,"
She spoke as one whose world is more a
    Theatre for the likes of her
Than an open field where sunlight falls
Or a fireside room within four walls.

And what she said was right—for Duse:
    She could distil a grief to a rapture
To fill a timeless urn, and use a
    Bitter despair again to capture
A glory to flame in a high control,
A pity to purge and sweeten the soul.

For Duncan and Duse these things were sure:
    Grief was a stuff to transmute and relume;
Elect and triumphant, they could endure
    A death and wring music out of the tomb;

They could refuse Time's balm, and be
Like silver trumpets in their agony.

But child of mine, I would not wish for you
Such gifts to bear as they, such work to do.
No, daughter, though you long to hug your grief
Best let Time steal it—he's a gentle thief.

THE road from Rocky Ford to Trinidad
Is always washing out, and then you take
A blind detour along the slopes to skirt
The wet arroyo that has lost its bridge.
On one of these, they came upon a car
Slewed in the ditch, and at the wheel a woman
Appealing to the passing world for help.
John stopped. The car, for all its coat of mud,
Was a long, custom-built, brown limousine,
And its rear wheels had spun until the axle
Was almost resting on the red ditch clay.
"Come on," the woman said, "and haul me out."
And April smiled at this magnificence
Appealing to a humble Model T.
"Have you a tow line?" "No, but haven't you?"
John shook his head. Just then a Mexican
Driving a wagon with a motley team,
A mule on near side, on the off a mare,
Her colt on a short lead. The Mexican
Stopped too, and sat like a carved walnut image;
The lad beside him grinned exultantly.
John went to him. His wagon-box was empty

But an old rope was tied across the tail-gate.
John borrowed it, explaining, though he got
No answer, taking silence for consent,
And as he finished tying it across
Between his axle and the shining bumper,
A bundle in the back seat came to life
And a moon face with silver hair reared up
And questioned gruffly, "What the hell you mean,
Waking me up? I told you just to wait."
The moon-faced man, once he disclosed himself,
Seemed with prodigious bulk to fill the car.
The woman said, "We can't sit here all day.
Get out. We never can move you." The man
Came slowly forth, a mountain of a man,
And stood and grumbled. John said, "Give her gas,"
And took a strain upon the rope. The Ford
Was on firm ground, and pulled courageously.
The boy got off the wagon, eyed the rope
And waited. But the woman missed her cue
For cigarette smoke in her eyes, and both
Her hands upon the wheel. The old rope snapped.
The Mexican said something to the boy
Who grinned, and jumped, and both the Ford's rear
     tires
Hissed out and flattened as the Mexican

Drove on, the boy, avenging knife in hand,
Climbing the tail-board. "Now I guess you'll wait,"
The fat man chuckled grimly. "Looka here,
I can't go back to sleep. You can't go on.
Let's have a game. You seem a gentleman."
He crawled back in the limousine, and swung
A shelf out from the seat-back for a table,
And opened a compartment, taking chips
And cards from it, and started dealing poker.
" 'Fraid I can't joint you," John said cautiously.
"I'll stake you," and the man detached a five
From a great roll, and counted out the chips.
"I've got to wait. But damned if I'll be bored."
The woman shrugged and lit a cigarette.
They played an hour. John's stack of chips was
        growing.
"Guess that'll do," the man said suddenly.
"Cash in. You've got enough to buy a pair
Of tires." He cashed, and folded up the table
And put the cards and chips away again.
Then he got out, looked at the drying ruts
In front of the half-buried wheels. "Now when,"
He said, "I holler, give her gas. No use
For any tow-rope. Just stand clear." He set
His mighty shoulder to the limousine,

And shouted, and his dame let in the clutch,
And the mud flew, the car's bulk heaved itself,
Like a great whale caught in an ebb lagoon,
Out of the ditch and landed on the road.
"So long, young fellow." The fat man climbed in.
"I'll send a man with tires from Trinidad.
But watch yourself. Don't borrow ropes. Don't try
To be a Galahad—it doesn't pay.
And one thing more. Out here your poker game
Is just another of the charities
You can't afford. You'll thank me, son,
If you live long enough, for that advice."
So John and April waited for the tires
To come, by a garage mechanic with
A sly and mocking smile, from Trinidad.

It's up the trail from Trinidad
I'd like to rise and go,
The trail the lean red oxen made
Long and long ago,
(And they made it very slow
'Mid the pine trees in the snow)
And it's up and up from Trinidad
(And the water laughs below)
That you twist and turn from grade to grade

And the sun beats down and the red rock's shade
Will put you in mind of the ambuscade
Of the prowling Navajo
What time the lean red oxen made
The pass in the long ago;
But it's up and up from Trinidad
That you'll climb and climb till you win a glad
Delight in a sight you'd sin a mad
Sin to be seeing away below—
For the trail that's up from Trinidad
Is the finest trail I know.

For it's there you look down across Ratoon
On a world of purple and gold,
And it spreads like the shimmer across the moon
And nothing to stop you, nothing to hold
From Wagon Mound to the Cimarroon
(The dust whirls dancing a rigadoon)
And the West lies wide to the Cimarroon
From the top of the mesa above Ratoon;
And it's there I'd rather be
Than in any town, New World or Old,
Or any port upon any sea,
And it's her I love I'd take with me,
On the best of days love ever had,

To the top of the trail from Trinidad
And look on the world of purple and gold
That you see from the mesa above Ratoon—
Mile on mile in the light unrolled—
And it's there we'd wait for the desert moon
To rise on the lands of the Cimarroon
(Look west—look west to the Cimarroon)
Till the ghostly oxen's ghostly gad
Drives them again from Trinidad
To the purple pastures below Ratoon;
And it's there my love and I would be
And listen and wait and kiss and see
Through the silent pines above Ratoon
The world lie still, and still lie we
Till the silver face of the desert moon
Would redden and sink over Cimarroon.
For the trail that's up from Trinidad
I'd choose to climb if I only had
One day more in the afternoon,
One night more beneath the moon.

THERE was a job, John heard around the plaza
In Santa Fe (and money running low),
Out past Cañada, up toward Rabbit Mountain;
You took the road along Bajada hill
Across to Cochiti, then bear northwest—
Well John and April knew the formula—
"You just can't miss it——" the great western lie;
But if there was a job, 'twas worth the gas,
And gas came high, here in New Mexico.
They took the old road over La Bajada,
And saw the mesas floating, step on step
Upward in purple to the Jemez peaks
The white sun etched in white against the blue.
The Ford crept downward on the rock-strewn curves
To the long flat below; and then they passed
The river, and a sound of drums and chanting
Blew on the wind from Cochiti. They listened
And turned along the river road. The square
At Cochiti was swept for festival.
Beside the drummer, chanting, moved the chorus,
Old men and young, in shirts of many colors,
And down the centre, skirting the brown pool

That gave back quick reflections of their bodies,
The dancers, masked as deer and buffalo,
With slender fore-leg sticks that tapped and tapped,
As they with stamping feet beat out the pattern;
And through the maze a maiden, shuffling slow
Like a still shadow imperturbable,
Threaded the figures. Epifanio
Was at the drum, and he could make it summon
The forest powers, the earth, the sky, the clouds
To give good hunting. Solemnly they trod
The ritual out, and when the drum beat ceased
The world stood still a moment. They knew then
That all the life behind them, all the roads
They'd ever travelled, all encounters past
Were swept as by a wind that blew afresh
Into their faces from this pulsing hour
Where a long past was beating up the future.
They sat a while in silence. Then John shook
Himself as if to break a spell too strong,
And turned away. He must inquire the road.
A gray-haired man with spectacles stood by
And John approached him. Yes, the dance was good.
It was a hunting dance. Great magic, too.
But you should see them when they dance for rain.
The road? Out by Cañada. Bear northwest—

But it winds in and out among the hills.
The gray man took a stick and drew a map
In the soft plaza dust. John studied it,
And thanked him vaguely, and they started on.
Through the first red and piñon-peppered hills
The track was clear enough, and mounted slowly
Along a sandy watercourse. They came to pines,
And then, beneath an overhanging cliff,
What seemed a town. They turned to it. Strange
    town
Was this Cañada. It had been a place
With a long plaza, and a belfried church
Stood midway down the square between the houses,
But now its roof was fallen, and the graves
In the walled churchyard overgrown with cactus.
One pale blue drift of piñon smoke came up,
Sweet-smelling, from a house that had not fallen,
And an old woman, shooing some white hens,
Like a brown wrinkled witch, stood by the door.
April went up to ask about the road:
Where, if you please, Señora, was Cañada?
The old crone grinned and showed her snag-toothed
    gums,
And answered in a flat midwestern voice,
This was Cañada—what was left of it—

And did they want to buy some eggs? She had
A dozen that were mighty fresh. And if
They'd buy 'em, she could get some meal—that is,
She could if they paid cash, and would be kind
To carry her up to the mill for it.
She lived alone there. Used to live before
In Albuquerque, but she found it lonesome.
This was Cañada—what about the eggs?
She talked, and John and April looked
Along the desolate sun-washed square, and up
To the high mesa overhanging it,
And never guessed the night of blood and storm
That swept it over, or the battle rage
That ruined it, twelve score of years ago,
The night Quintana brought his people through
The arrows to the walls of Santa Fe;
Nor could they see, upon the mesa top
The ruins of that older city where
The snows a thousand winters deep had thawed
Since last the drums they heard at Cochiti
Had beaten for the hunting festivals. . . .
Yes, they would take the eggs. The woman brought
     them
In a tin can. John paid her. She got in
And started for the mill. She warn't alone,

She said, there in Cañada. "There's a no-account
Old cowhand up from Texas—he camps there.
But I've no truck with such as him. His language
Is something awful when he's had a drink;
Or when he hasn't—I can't figger which.
But he goes his way, and I mind my knittin'.
Yender's the mill. I'm very much obliged."
They stopped. The mill, a tiny hut, adobe
With rough foundation of red stone, and roofed
With mud above a plaited willow ceiling
Gave out a sleepy sound, a thump, thump, thump
Of the old wooden wheel, a tinkling splash
Of water from the mossy blades of it,
And a low rumble of the whirling stone.
The miller, a dark, one-eyed Mexican,
Sat by the door, flour-whitened as all millers
Should be. "Yender's your road up to that ranch."
They passed two homesteads. Then they came to
    gates
In a stone wall, as some great hacienda
Might well be guarded, and drove in. The house
Was rambling, larger, richer in its air
Than they expected. And a silent lad,
Alert, with hostile, somehow frightened eyes,

Admitted John. The master of the house
Sat in a huge old pigskin chair. Beside
Him, on a beaten silver tray, were glasses
And a half-empty bottle of old brandy.
A man not easily approachable,
Dressed in the height of what the eastern mind
Might well design for such a place and state.
The man was young, with brooding sullen brows
Hard drawn, and all the spring gone out of him.
"You came to see about a job? Hell, no,
I don't want anybody. Never will, I guess.
Last week I may have mentioned it. The plant
For our electric lights was on the blink
And I sent down for someone who could keep
The thing in order. These damned Mexicans——
But now I don't need anything." He paused,
And took another drink. "My wife has left.
Pulled out. She said she couldn't stand it here
Another day. But I'll be doubled damned
If I go back." He drank again. "Move on.
I can't be bothered." . . . And John took his leave.

Coronado came on horseback,
Long and loud his trumpets blew

107

(But he couldn't hear the flute notes),
And his iron armor clattered
And the wary red folk scattered
Where his haughty banners flew.
(But he couldn't hear the mute notes
That had died before the flute notes—
Couldn't hear and never knew.)

General Kearney came with snare drums
And with bugles blowing strong
(But he couldn't hear the vespers),
And he made prophetic speeches
All of peace, as history teaches,
For his flag could do no wrong;
(But he couldn't hear the vespers,
Couldn't hear the quiet vespers'
Never ending evensong.)

Now you come with eights and sixes,
Brakes that squeal and horns that blow
(But you'll never hear the silence),
And the lizards know you're coming
When they hear your motors humming
And your gears go into low.
(But you'll never hear the silence—

Far too wide the desert silence,
Far too still the mountain silence
Ever such as you to know.)

Better sound your horn and go.

ALONG the road that passed the mill they found
The crone just starting homeward with her flour.
They picked her up. "It's getting late," she said.
"You may as well stay here. You'll never find
Your way back in the dark." And so they stayed,
Sleeping beneath their blankets in a house
With the roof gone, the swarming sky above.
When morning came, John foraged for some wood
To cook a breakfast, down among the ruins,
And in the rubbish he picked up a slab
Of ancient oak; he was about to split
The panel—tapped it to knock off the dust—
And saw that it was painted. Absently
He brushed it off. The weathered painting still
Showed clear: a giant wading through a stream
With Christ a child upon his mighty shoulders.
John took it in the house and set it up.
The old crone came in cackling, just to see
If they had what they'd need for breakfast. "So,"

She crowed, "you've found one. What they call a
    santos.
I used to burn no end of them for firewood,
But now I save 'em. There's a man from town
Will give a quarter for 'em." April came
And reverently cleaned the face of it.
"Saint Christopher—the saint of travellers,"
She said. "He's not for sale. We might be wise
To pray his intercession." "Cath'lic trash,"
The old crone answered. "But I never seen
One just like this. It might be worth a dollar.
You'd better sell." "Not while we're travellers,"
And April stowed the panel in the car.
They started when the sun was high, but lost
The road, and wandered, miles, it seemed
Beneath the pines, until they came again
To what had been, in other years, a town;
Not like the others; first a square of stonework,
Eyeless and roofless, and above the door,
Cut in the lintel, the word "Bank." And on,
Upward the gulch, were false-front wooden stores
Deserted. Then a crushing mill, its slant
Of iron roof one slant of rust; inside,
A rusted huddle of great iron wheels,
And tanks for cyanide, all rusted out;

Above, the open shaft mouth and an ore dump;
Here was a mine—a gold mine—all abandoned.
John stopped the car. This thing must be explored.
He clambered up the ore dump to the mouth
Of the dark shaft. Then from the trail below
A passer-by in greasy overalls
Hailed him. "You'd better not go in. She's cavin';
Old timberin' is rotted down. 'Taint safe."
The man went on. John could not leave the place.
They camped that night beside the ghost-town Bank,
And April set Saint Christopher beside
The tent-flap; they had never thought, till then,
That they were travellers and might need a saint
To be their guardian. Before they went
To sleep, from a long stillness, April spoke.
"She must be crazy." "Who?" "That rancher's wife
Who said she couldn't stand it here." They lay
On the hard ground and let their minds run back
Along the year. Somehow the film broke off
At Ratoon pass. The films from farther east
Would never flicker on these older walls,
These simpler, warmer mud-built walls and stone.
Yes, they were travellers. Saint Christopher
Looked down on them with gentle painted eyes,
And blessed them, more than likely, as they slept.

Cybele the Earth lies armored and mailed
     Afar in the east, in the cities,
And her children are hard and their spirits are scaled
     With sequins to smother their pities,
And our Mother the Earth is ashamed of a race
That never takes joy to be seeing her face.

Cybele the Earth in the Middle West
     Is fat and she goes in a garment of green,
And her hills are as smooth as a rounded breast,
     And in autumn she walks like a gilded queen,
And even in winter she wears the snows
Softer than ermine wherever she goes.

But here she is naked and lean and the sun
     Will be burning, the winds will be blowing her
        hair,
And the granite grace of her skeleton
     Will be showing through where her shoulder's
        bare,
And her brows are forbidding, her dreaming eyes
Are gazing above where the eagle flies.

Our Mother the Earth in the Sangre de Christo
     Is a passionate sorceress luring the stars,

And the stars have come down in the Sangre de
  Christo
  And their kisses have marked her with mystical
  scars.

And either you love her, body and bone,
Or you hate her and leave her . . . dreaming alone.

THE trouble is," John said, "this prospecting
Has a technique, a trick, and we don't know it.
We'd better get a book." In Albuquerque
They found a store, "BOOKS, New and Second
    Hand,"
But money was by that time almost gone,
And they proposed a trade. You never get
Your value for a book in trade, and theirs
Were books of verse—the hardest books to sell—
The hardest too to part with. Keats and Shelley
Went for a volume titled *Placer Mining,*
A Guide for Prospectors. No easy trade,
But when the devil drives, needs must. They might
Have made a better deal if they would sell
Saint Christopher, but April flat refused;
He might bring luck, and luck is what you need
In prospecting. She spent a half a day
There in the Public Library, reading up,
While John put in his time along the streets
Hearing a parcel of tall western tales
Of long lost mines, and strikes in far off gulches,
And knowing all the while the tales were lies,

For in that year there was no end of talk
Of gold and silver, turquoise, lead and mica,
And how the teller always knew a man
Who knew another man who found his fortune,
Although he never knew just how, or where.
But in the stories came and came again
The ranges to the south—San Andres Mountains,
And so that night they headed south. The Ford
Was none too sturdy; better strike it near.
They passed Isleta Indians at work
In the old network of prayer-guarded ditches,
Each man a selfless unit in the tribe's
Long heritage of toil. They passed Los Lunas
And smelled the piñon smoke and saw the women
Black-shawled and silent coming from the church.
They saw the black cones of volcanic ash
Upon the right, to left the Rio Grande,
And far beyond, against the sun, Sandia,
Alone and loveliest of the sacred peaks,
Shaped for the Turtle who had reared the land
Out of the sea in the creation song.
Beyond Socorro, midway of the stretch
Of fourscore miles that had no towns at all
They came upon a halted car. The man
With spectacles, the gray and dusty man

They'd seen at Cochiti, had the hood off
And tinkered hopefully the carburetor;
His wife, gray too but young about the eyes,
Sat at the wheel and tried from time to time
What the foiled spark would do. John stopped the
    Ford,
(April said something about Galahad)
And went to offer help. The gray-haired man
Had fingers stained with ink and paint, and now
Blackened with grease. The car was loaded down
With camping gear, and old and daubed sketch boxes,
And it had too a shovel tied across
Its bumper rod. John tried his hand. No luck.
"There is a mystery," the man observed,
"About a car. My generation finds
It very baffling. Yours was born to it,
And you may know what spring to touch, what spell
To speak." They took the thing apart, for John,
By this time roused, would not admit defeat.
The woman left the wheel and went to April
And smiled and said, "This looks like a long job,
And I suggest we get a lunch for them.
I have the makings." She and April spread
A cloth on a flat rock, and from a box,
An old black box among the sketching traps,

They flourished forth the noon repast. A truck
Laden with pale rock from some mine to westward
Made trips down to a flat-car by the river
And back again, the driver never pausing
To see what might be done for charity.
They ate the lunch, and laughed and talked somehow
More freely than they'd laughed in all the year
Before. In this gray couple's eyes they found
Something the road had never given back
In all its chance encounters, until now.
These people asked no questions, but they seemed
To know the drift, and John and April poured
Their spirits out as in a mother's lap.
The car had baffled them. The sun hung low
When the truck-driver, back from his last trip,
Took pity. "Looka here," he said, "there ain't
A place to stop for forty miles. I'm headed
Down to Hot Springs. I'll give you-all a push,"
And so he did. The gray man rode with John
In the hard-driven Ford, which they filled up
With gas drawn from the useless reservoir
Of the disgraced sedan called "Ariadne,"
While April joined the woman with young eyes
And watched the road for her. It was a task
To meet the long road's windings with the truck

Pounding behind them, pushing Ariadne,
And so they came to Hot Springs in the dark,
And by that time, there seemed no casual way
For them to part. The woman with young eyes
Invited them to dine and stay the night
In the hotel, and John and April slept
In such a comfort as they had forgotten.

"It's strange," John said, "we've met so many people
But not like these." "Our own, somehow," said April.
"They might have been your parents." "Yes, or
    yours."
In the still morning, Ariadne, mended,
Warmed up her engine underneath their window.
"They're getting off," John cried. "We didn't say
Goodbye." But April in her dressing gown
Was halfway down stairs by the time he said it,
And caught the woman with the youthful eyes
Around the neck. "You wouldn't slip away
Without . . . without . . . " and April kissed her
    hard
And clung to her. "We wouldn't make a sneak,"
The gray man disavowed. "We wanted breakfast.
But if you're ready, come for coffee too."
And after breakfast, Ariadne swung

To northward, and goodbyes were said,
And John and April never saw again
The gray man and the woman with young eyes.

That's how we met you,
April and John,
And we couldn't forget you
The road we were on;

And the story you told us
Just with your eyes
Was a glow to enfold us,
And if there are lies
In the book I am making
It's no fault of yours,
It's my word I'm breaking—
Your stuff endures.

For it's one thing to write of it—
(Maybe I'm wrong)
But yours was the flight of it,
Yours was the song;
You put the youth in it,
I put the rhymes,
Yours was the truth in it—
Mine are the crimes.

I couldn't make light of you,
*   Youth and your dreams,*
Youth and the might of you—
*   God, how it seems*
As though it were yesterday
*   We were like you—*
Life at its Easterday
*   Calling us too.*

Yes, you looked fine to us;
*   Just* entre nous
You were like wine to us:
*   Were we to you*
Old wine from a bottle
*   Not without zest*
As you opened the throttle
*   And turned to the west?*

You were too kind to us—
*   If you but knew—*
Ah, but you signed to us
*   Love that was true*
The day that we met you,
*   April and John,*
And we couldn't forget you,
*   The road we were on.*

THEY went with Getch because Getch was a
   miner;
Getch went with them because they had a Ford,
And he had traded his old horse for grub,
New boots and shot-gun shells and blankets,
And had no other way to pack his stuff
From Hot Springs over to San Andres Mountains.
Getch did not talk much on the way across;
Around the curve where the road spanned the dam,
While John and April marvelled at the blue
Clear depths around the Elephant, the whiteness
Of the straight yucca spears, and the sharp fire
That shaped the buttes to eastward in the sun,
Getch only said, "There's water here. The trouble
In the San Andres is there ain't none there.
These mountains, they don't seem to hold no snow."
Getch was no optimist, to hear him tell it,
And yet the trade he followed was sheer hope.
"A horse, now, you can turn him loose. He'll find
The water. This here car—*you* have to find it.
It's hell—but this is what we've got. At that,
I have a mind to look them gulches over."

Across a flat of clean white sand that turned

To blue where the long shadows fell, they saw,

Gold red, and laced with opaque purple gorges,

The range of the San Andres. As the trail

Grew rougher, the last tracks ran out;

They camped. Next morning they worked further up

Till it was plain the Ford had reached the end

Of its ascent. They found a spring, put up

The tent, and then Getch took command. "From here,"

He said, "we'll pack our pans. You'll be all right

Here in the camp, and, Missus, we'll go up

And squint these gulches till we find some color."

So April waited, and they went. To John

At first the pack seemed light enough. He followed,

And tried to bring to mind the smattering

Of such geology as he had learned

In school, and the pat phrases of the *Guide*

For Prospectors—but all the time he felt

Old Getch the desert rat would smell out gold

Before he could apply the recipe,

(Forgetting that old Getch had sold his horse

For grub enough to make just one more try).

But Getch was blind to seams and faults and gravel,

And only bent on finding in some gully

Water enough to fill his pan. But when
They found a pool, Getch came alive, and spun
The gravel, sending John to climb the slopes
And bring in samples. So three days went by,
Three lonesome nights, and cold, for all the fires
They heaped before they went to sleep. And John
Each night looked up and found the Lyre, and
    thought
Of April back there in the tent alone.
On the fourth day, Getch found one yellow grain,
And cursed a while, and then sat down and looked
Across the pan at John. His pale blue eyes
Were blank and quite expressionless.
He sat and thought, and looked down on the valley,
And thought some more, his rough hands very still.
"This gulch," he said at last, "has water in it,
And it might yield six bits a day. We'll stop
And pan a little here before we go
On up the mountains. You go back to camp
And tell your Missus. Yes, and take her this."
He wrapped the grain of gold in some tinfoil
He tore from a tobacco packet. "Lookee,
Ye needn't hurry. I'll be here all right.
But fetch up all the grub ye can." John took
The precious grain and set off down the gulch.

Landmarks were few. They had not blazed their trail.
It was next day at noon when he found April,
And sat with her, and passed the yellow grain
From hand to hand. Six bits a day, old Getch
Had said; but then, Getch was no optimist.
And if there were six bits, why not a million?
The book said—but why trust the book when they
Had Getch himself, a seasoned prospector,
For partner? "Curious," April mused, "we take
His word, we trust——" "But he found gold," John
   urged,
And had a twinge of conscience—he had left
Her there alone—no wonder she was not
So fired with hope and confidence as he.
He started back, and for the first long march
April went with him, lugging half his load,
And noting landmarks, for each rusty shoulder
Of the long range was like the next. Then she
Turned back to guard the camp, and he went on,
His burden doubled. It was nearly night
When he approached their gulch, and saw the smoke
Of Getch's campfire. Just below the tall
Red rock that marked the opening of the gulch,
He found three horses tethered, their backs marked
With sweat from heavy packs. John came around

The rock. Old Getch sat still, his shot-gun laid
Across his knees. Another man, a short
Squat man was at the pool. "Don't come no further,"
Getch challenged sternly. "This here claim is staked—
Due form of law. And stranger, you stop there,
Right where ye be." The short, squat man stood up
And moved to stand by Getch. John laughed, and
        dropped
His pack. "All right, but you will have to come
And get the victuals, partner." "We'll do that,"
The short man answered, "jest you leave 'em there."
Old Getch leaned over and spat out his quid,
And said, "You better go. I never said
That me and you was pardners. My old pardner,
He's here with me to hold this claim." He stood,
And John could see his new boots were in shreds
About his feet. And then John saw a light.
He made no threats. He just said "Damn your soul,"
For form's sake, and went down the trail.
He knew it well enough by this time. When
The moon came up, he still could follow it,
And in the dawn he sighted April's tent.
She only said, "I had my doubts of him,"
And took John in her arms. The Ford had gas

Enough to take them to the dam again.
They bought two gallons at the fishing tavern,
And landed at Hot Springs with ninety cents,
And with some first-hand information on
The subject, general and particular,
Of Placer Mining, not in any book.

There's gold in the hills: any fool can find it,
But what does it pay for his labor and pain?
Some corporation will come and grind it,
Some soulless cartel with cyanide
Will muscle in and the fool can ride
Off to the glimmering hills again.

So if you were born with more hope than sense,
And can live on a gleam and a side of bacon,
Load up your mule (at your own expense)
And tighten your belt, and when you're
athirst
You can suck at a cactus, and know that the
worst
Is still to come and the best forsaken.

But your job is as lucky as mine, my lad,
It has the seal of Apollo upon it;

You'll be combing the golden gulches like mad,
And I will be hammering bolts to be hurled,
In a crazy design to be lashing the world
With the futile sting in the tail of a sonnet.

THE husky Dane who packed the patients in
The mud at the Excelsior Baths was down
With rheumatism, and John got his job,
And the first patient that he had to pack
Was Jesus M. Delgado with arthritis.
John could not know, with Jesus groaning there
In the warm mud, and trying as he might
To keep his gray mustache from being daubed,
That he was lord of ranges wider than
The State of Delaware, and that his word
Was law to men who watched ten thousand sheep;
John only knew he tipped him fifty cents,
And so he rated lower in John's scale
Than the El Paso bird who tipped a dollar.
When in three weeks the husky Dane came back,
They had a grubstake, and a line, red hot,
Upon the gold in the Mogollon Mountains.
They took the road again, determined now
To find their fortune with no counsellor
To guide and share. (The bitter gleam of gold
Is acid to the metal of your trust

In the fair-seeming face of humankind.)
To north and westward, on a two-rut road,
They worked away from the slow Rio Grande,
And upward on the mesas where the flowers
Upon the spidery ocatillos flamed
With rose-red petals against rust red earth,
And higher, where the tortured lava flow,
All black and brittle, broke along the hills,
And upward still to where they saw the snows
Of the Mogollons. There each gully seemed,
Until they panned their samples, the trail's end.
At last they found some color in the pan,
And stopped, and set the tent, and made a camp.
The wash that day (there was a spring not far
Where they could get fresh water) yielded up
Three grains of gold, the largest not so big
As half a wheat grain, but they welcomed it
With shouts as though it were Dame Fortune's
    nugget.
And when dark fell, they lay and watched the stars.
They found bright Vega, but she seemed to them
Like a queen bee surrounded by her swarm,
And all the constellations in this air,
So clear and dustless, seemed to have come down
Nearer and million-fold more intimate.

This night a year ago, they lay beneath
The trees and looked up at the sky:
They were the same, and love was still the same,
And yet within them was a change like that
In the cold fires above them. For their life
Was fuller as this sky was fuller now
Than it had been. They had come far. They had
Three grains of gold. And as their minds ran back
Along the year, they knew these grains of gold
For what they really were. That night that crowned
The year of pilgrimage they knew was marked
With gold their three soft grains could never buy.

Next morning, John set up his stakes
And wrote his notices and tacked them up,
And they broke camp and headed down the gulch
To register their claim. The way was rough,
And they were not so watchful now. They'd come
To the trail's end. They waited for a flock,
An endless flock it seemed, of pouring sheep,
Slow driven to the upper mountain pastures;
And they looked back to see the shepherds close,
Wary and patient, lest the flock should break
At the loud rattle of the Ford—looked back
A moment—and the car's wheels bumped and veered

And in a slithering crash went down a draw
And staggered, and turned over, and lay still.

When John came to, he found a million sheep
A-march, and menacing before his eyes
That could not be quite sure if they were sheep
Or stabbing shapes of pain. He was enmeshed
Pinioned beneath the broken car. His sight
Grew clearer, and he dragged himself, with one
Slow surge of all his strength, from out the wreck.
April lay still, her left arm twisted strangely
Beneath her head, and blood along the arm.
John shook with a dull sobbing, called to her,
And tried to rise and reach her; heard a shout,
Looked up, and saw on horseback on the ridge
A man, who touched his horse's side with spurs,
And came. A man who seemed, there on the horse,
Just what he was, the lord of a great range,
And after him, four shepherds ran along
To take his bidding. As the man dismounted
John knew he was no stranger, this great man,
With gray mustache, and rich and kindly voice.
The shepherds lifted John, and let him feel
His weight upon his legs. Yes, he could stand.
The master of the cordon went to April,

And gently straightened out the broken arm,
And laid her head back, and with his sombrero
Fanned her white face until her eyelids fluttered.
He turned with sharp authority to one,
The oldest of the shepherds, and gave orders,
Swiftly and low, in Spanish. Then to John
He spoke in English. "She's not hurt, I think,
Except the broken arm. My man can make
A splint to hold it till I get a doctor."
And to the shepherd, one more word of haste.
The shepherd bowed and said, "*Si, Don Jesus.*"

Swiftly the shepherd cut and split and whittled
A piece of soft white yucca wood, and gently
Pulled the arm straight and bound it. April lay
And followed with her glance his surgery,
And set her lips, and when the man stood up
She smiled and whispered, "*Gracias, Señor,*"
And with the words she made a friend for life,
Though speaking them had taken all her Spanish,
Of Tranquillino, the head Caporal.
John somberly surveyed the wreck, and knew
If he had all the junk heaps left in Kansas,
He could not make it run again. That Ford
Had a great heart, but now its beat was done.

A wagon came. Don Jesus gave directions.
They lifted April, and spread all the blankets,
And put the half-rolled tent beneath her head,
And Tranquillino made a sort of sling
To keep the arm from jolting. Don Jesus
Stood smiling as they made a common pack
Of all the small possessions from the Ford,
And nodded shrewdly when he saw the books
And the surveying tools. "I see," he said.
"By what you have, I know you very well."
The shepherds crossed themselves when they took up
Saint Christopher, split cleanly in his fall,
And paused to tie the broken parts together;
When he was mended properly, they said,
He should be blessed again; but as they spoke
In Spanish only, John made nothing of it.
And then deliberately Don Jesus
Gave orders to the Caporal. To John
He also spoke: "I send you to the ranch.
A doctor will come soon. Care will be taken
Of her. And you. My Caporal will see
That you want nothing." Then he paused and smiled.
"Nothing, I mean, that my poor house can furnish.
I saw you once before—remember you.
You were not doing what you might have wished—

But better luck hereafter." At his elbow
A man brought up his horse; Don Jesus mounted.
"One moment," John said. "I am not ungrateful,
But I need one thing more." Don Jesus waited.
"We cannot move to leave your house—that's plain.
But I can work. If you will tell them that——"
"Just as you please, John. That's the name
You told me at the bath-house, is it not?
I will tell Tranquillino. He is head
Of all the ranch while I am absent. Now,
I must go on. My flocks are moving up,
And it's an anxious time with us." He wheeled,
And lifted his sombrero in salute
To April where she lay, said "*Adios*,"
And rode away, his shepherds at his heels.

> *What do you see, Shepherd Pablo,*
> *Nights, when the sheep move slow?*
> *See stars and maybe a wolf's green eye*
> *Catch fire from my fire glow.*

> *And do you not fear, Shepherd Pablo,*
> *In the hills where the wolves run free?*
> *I have no need for to be afraid—*
> *Patron, he look after me.*

And what do you think, Shepherd Pablo?
    You surely must have some idea—
Maybe next month I go off the range
    On Sunday, and walk with Maria.

And what do you want, Shepherd Pablo,
    And what is life's meaning to you?
I want for no hombre come talking at me—
    One man not so lonesome as two.

When you lie on your back, Shepherd Pablo,
    Looking up so, what do you see?
See Patron look after the stars himself;
    He leave the sheep to me.

ABOUT the rancho things were always done
As they had always been. No need for change.
Old Roybalita always baked her bread
In a clay oven; always cooked the beans
With chili as her mother must have done;
And on a feast day always served roast kid.
At first John felt that they were guests, and served
As guests, because the patron ordered so.
They set themselves to learn some Spanish
And the old woman humored April with it,
Chuckling and grunting over her mistakes,
And April soon began to understand
The simple household words; the hardest part
Was learning the more necessary things—
The courtesies, and Roybalita gave
Her scant encouragement in this; was it
Polite to be correcting the Señora's manners,
The patron's orders being what they were?
John persevered to make himself of use,
And Tranquillino, grudgingly at first,
Accepted him as one more pair of hands.
The word came down to fence the breeding pastures

And make them larger, for the count was good,
And new corrals for lambs. "You make good fence,"
Was Tranquillino's pristine approbation,
Passed on, in English, by a grave-eyed boy
Who had attached himself to John to learn
More English. Then a funeral group came in
With a dead man who had been killed by lightning,
And John went up the range with Tranquillino
To count the flock and give them into charge
Of a new Caporal. John made the count
Twelve hundred seven, Tranquillino found
Twelve hundred four—and all to do again.
But John was right, and the old foreman glowered
Until they reached the ranch. "You make good count,"
He said at last, and smiled a little, kindly.
That night they talked, and the dark boy translated,
With April sitting by—good chance to learn,
When the translation followed on the words.
"You, Señor John," he said, "will never get
To be a sheep herd. No. You think not right
For watching flock. You'll never learn. You'll think
The sheep they think what no sheep ever thinks.
You never can be slow enough. You have
No head for work with flock. But I like you,

And like Señora. Do not wish discourage.
You make good count, and that is mos' important.
You can't be sheep herd. . . . You might be patron."
John thanked him with much courtesy for these
Kind words, regretting inabilities;
The boy translated conscientiously,
And Tranquillino bowed. "So we be friends.
I never meant to be discourage', but
A man must say the truth. What sort of work
You do before you come here?" "Counted people,
Once, for the Government." "I see. That's good.
Our patron, he is Government. He go,
In winter, far, to Washington. Go soon,
For Congress. But he mainly go in winter.
Ver' good to work for Government. I thought—
Beg you forgive—you might be prospector."
And Tranquillino's face went cold and hard.
"You don't like prospectors?" "Not quite so well
As I like wolves. One prospector will steal
More sheep than a whole family of wolves.
They kill for nothing—just to cut one chop.
No, they are bad." "Not all of them," said April.
"You ever know one good?" They thought of Getch,
The only one they knew, and dropped the matter.
"I find gold once," the Caporal went on,

"Big piece, wire gold, like lizard made of gold.
Take him to town. Man give me twenty dollar.
What I remember mos', I wake in jail
And my head very sore. Now, I find gold,
I give him Roybalita for to keep
In old tobacco bag. She think some day
She spend for masses for which one of us
Die first. That way, maybe, gold not so bad.
But people don' need gold. Need meat and wool,
Need food and clothes. It's better we tend sheep.
Look here. You stay five year. You learn to be
One good patron. You make straight fence. You
count.
When you are older, men will work for you.
Then you file homestead. . . . I would work for you,
If my patron not want me any more."
And April, without waiting for the boy,
In her best Spanish, told old Tranquillino,
"You are one good man, and one man most wise.
I pray to God to spare Don Jesus long,
But if you leave this house, you come to us."
"*Señora, gracias,*" Tranquillino said,
And stood, and made a bow that was a pledge
Of faith as long as he should live, as if

The intervening chances of the years
Were nothing, and the work to do that night.

You counted the people, and never knew
What the people were like that you counted,
And the old died off and the children grew
To put you out as your totals mounted.

And once you were anxiously counting your money,
And when it was gone, the anxious hours;
But now you'll be measuring mountain honey
Your own bees store from the mountain flowers.

Now you'll harden your hands on the pick and shovel,
And you'll break your backs till you prove your
claim,
And you'll live at first in a canvas hovel,
For the proving up is a difficult game.

And you'll puddle your mud and you'll count your
bricks
As they bake in the sun, and you'll build you a
house,
And to hell with these corrugated tricks—
You'll roof it with earth upon cedar boughs.

And you'll lay a fire on your own hearthstone,
     And you'll kindle it with a useless book;
And you won't be sitting before it alone,
     For a friend will come with a shepherd's crook

And bring you a santos to hang above—
     A San Ysidro, saint of the sod,
To guard your flocks and guard your love
     And to intercede when you go to God.

And you'll count your sheep on your grazing land
     (For the wolves will get some, and the rot a few)
But the spring will your losses countermand
     When the ewes drop one or the ewes drop two.

And your children will gather about your fire
     And sing in the twilight, a shrill quartette,
And the wind will blow from your chimney spire
     The piñon smell that you can't forget.

And when the work of the day is done
     You will go out and be counting the stars,
And the night will murmur with brooks that run,
     And your shepherds strumming their old guitars.

And the constellations will keep their round
And Vega burn and the years run on:
And what could I wish you you haven't found?
So hail and farewell to you, April and John.